EMPLOYMENT LAW
in Agriculture and Estate Management

Peter Morris

Royal Agricultural University
Cirencester

PACKARD PUBLISHING LIMITED
CHICHESTER

EMPLOYMENT LAW
in Agriculture and Estate Management

© 2021 David Peter Morris

First published in the United Kingdom, 2021, by Packard Publishing Ltd, 14 Guilden Road, Chichester, West Sussex, PO19 7LA, UK.

This short book corresponds to its equivalent chapter in the fifth revised edition of *Land and Estate Management*, 2021.

ISBN 978-1-85341-158-8 paperback only.

A CIP catalogue record of this book is available from the British Library.

Prepared for press by Michael Packard.

Front-cover and title page photo courtesy of Carter Jonas.

Layout and design by Hilite Design, Marchwood, Southampton, Hampshire.

Printed and bound in the UK by Lemonade Print Group, Burgess Hill, West Sussex.

Contents

Acknowledgements

I would like to thank Sara Cohen, Partner at Lewis Silkin, Solicitors, London, for her advice and help, and Rachael Lloyd, Senior Associate at Michelmores, Solicitors.

D. P. M

EMPLOYMENT LAW
in agriculture and estate management

The last 25 years have seen a major change in the laws and regulations relating to employment. There has been a significant amount of legislation that applies in general to employment in the United Kingdom but given the nature of agriculture, there have been some laws and regulations that are specific to that industry. For example, the Agricultural Wages Board, which was set up in 1948 to regulate the pay of workers in agriculture, was effectively abolished in England in 2013. The Board had played a significant part in maintaining and ensuring minimum terms and wages for agricultural workers. To this must be added the effect of the considerable number of regulations in the form of Directives created by the European Union and the application of the provisions of the Human Rights Act 1998.

Agriculture has seen a reduction in the number of people working in it over a sustained period, with most farms now having only two or three people working on them – if that. This is evidenced by figures from the Office for National Statistics which show that from the nineteenth century to 2011 the percentage of people in the UK employed in agriculture has dropped from 33 to one per cent[1].

Suffice it to say that wide-reaching effects of employment law in the UK need to be addressed by all employers, and it is worthwhile to seek specialised advice if there is any doubt about the correct procedure when dealing with employment rights. Failure to follow the correct procedure can result in

---

[1] www.ons.gov.uk/ons/rel/census/2011-census-analysis/170-years-of-industry/170-years-of-industrial-changeponent.html

successful claims against employers (on technical grounds), and seeking specialist advice early can often avoid extra costs through unnecessary expenditure and the breakdown of goodwill.

Again, as with other industries, the two key institutions that affect employment in the agricultural sector are Employment Tribunals and The Advisory, Conciliation and Arbitration Service (ACAS). It is important to know the terms of reference for these two institutions and the possible help they can give and sanctions they can impose.

EMPLOYMENT TRIBUNALS

The essence of such a tribunal is that it was set up to be more informal than a court of law and to be less costly to the participants. However, because of the complexity of the rules and regulations relating to employment law that have developed over the years, the presence of solicitors and barristers has become commonplace making a tribunal a potentially expensive forum in which to be involved. It should be noted that under the Employment Tribunals (Constitution and Rules of Procedure) Regulations 2013 (known as the '2013 Regulations'), and by Regulation 76(1), an order for costs may be made when a Tribunal considers that:

(a) a party (or that party's representative) has acted vexatiously, abusively, disruptively or otherwise unreasonably in either the bringing of the proceedings (or part) or the way that the proceedings (or part) have been conducted; or (b) any claim or response had no reasonable prospect of success.

There is a time-limit for claiming costs of 28 days following the date of the judgment (Regulation 76 (5)).

The constitutional basis of the employment tribunal is the Employment Tribunals Act 1996, which did away with the previous label of 'industrial tribunals'. Employment tribunals' jurisdiction naturally covers the majority of disputes concerning matters of employment, but the extent of their jurisdiction has widened when the rules and regulations affecting employment increased to include matters of equality, discrimination, harassment, maternity and paternity rights, working hours, part-time and flexible working and safety matters. Each area should be addressed to see what the terms of reference are to an employment tribunal.

A tribunal can consist of an employment judge and two lay members but, in many cases, including claims for unfair dismissal, an employment judge can sit alone. They will be either a barrister or a solicitor; other members are selected from panels and are appointed after consultation with employers' and employees' organisations, for example trade unions. The 2013 Regulations set out inter alia the procedure, the management of cases before a tribunal and the legal remedies that a tribunal can award at the end of a hearing.

The decision will sometimes be delivered on the day of hearing but the tribunal has the power to reserve judgement. By Regulation 61(1) the judgment must then be sent in writing to the parties 'as soon as is practicable'.

Appeals can be made resulting from the decision of an employment tribunal to an Employment Appeal Tribunal (EAT). An appeal in such circumstances must be on a point of law, and under the Regulations 2A (1) of the Employment Appeal Tribunal Rules 1993 (as amended) the overriding objective of which is to 'deal with cases justly'. The factors to effect this are equal footing for the parties, proportionality, dealing with cases expeditiously and to save expense. The EAT consists of High Court judges sitting with lay members who are considered by the Lord Chancellor and the Secretary of State to have special knowledge or experience of industrial relations and disputes. Thereafter appeals are to the Court of Appeal, again on a point of law, with the leave of the EAT.

ADVISORY, CONCILIATION AND ARBITRATION SERVICE

This service is more commonly known as 'ACAS'. It was given statutory foundation in 1975 under the Employment Protection Act. Its overarching objective is to promote and by advice to improve industrial relations. ACAS has since its inception established several areas of working practice that have avoided the need for conflict. To fulfil its objective, its officers advise organisations by visiting their premises, talking to the various people involved, carrying out surveys and organizing joint working parties. This work is supplemented by a number of leaflets and brochures.

The second element of the work done by ACAS is conciliation. ACAS can by its own initiative, or by request of an interested party, attempt to achieve some form of conciliation. ACAS employs conciliation officers who are commissioned to secure conciliation in matters that could otherwise go to tribunals. Often conflicts can be resolved at an early stage by the process of a mandatory 'Early Conciliation' by an ACAS officer.

If the conciliation officer fails to bring about agreement, the matter goes to an employment tribunal. Any information given to the conciliation officer is confidential and is not admissible in tribunal proceedings.

Under Section 20 of the Employment Rights Act 1996 (ERA), any conciliatory agreement reached through the involvement of a conciliation officer will be legally binding. Generally employees cannot surrender their statutory rights, and so the involvement of ACAS can certainly be an effective and less costly method of resolving issues of employment. ACAS is also responsible for drafting Codes of Practice to supplement its work, the most important being at the time of writing the Disciplinary and Grievance Procedure ('Grievance Procedure') which is important when considering the dismissal of an employee.

GANGMASTER'S REGULATION

In 2004, 20 migrant workers drowned in the sea at Morecambe Sands in Lancashire when gathering shellfish. The workers were under the control of gangmasters, and they were working in the UK illegally. The gangmaster involved was jailed afterwards for a period of 14 years for manslaughter.

Following the tragedy, and as a result, the employment and use of workers was regulated under the terms of the Gangmasters (Licensing) Act 2004 which came into force on 1 April 2005. This was modified by the Gangmasters Licensing (Exclusions) Regulations 2013. In short, the Act was established to avoid exploitation of workers in agriculture, horticulture, shellfish gathering and associated procedures and packaging sectors. Section 3 (3) of the 2004 Act sets out a detailed list of the activities included in the definition of 'agriculture'.

The 2004 Act created the Gangmaster Licensing Authority by its Section 1. The Authority's powers extend to granting licences to persons qualifying under the terms of the Act, and appointing 'compliance officers' who monitor the activities of the licensed gangmasters. By Section 15 the Home Secretary has power to appoint 'enforcement officers' who will enforce the 'prohibition of activities' of acting as an unlicensed gangmaster under Section 6 of the 2004 Act and the offences set out in Sections 12, 13 and 14, which also include acting as an unlicensed gangmaster.

In 2016, the Immigration Act 2016 renamed the Gangmaster Licensing Authority as the Gangmasters and Labour Abuse Authority and extended its powers.

APPOINTING EMPLOYEES

The appointment of employees is an important part of any business, but among the typically small rural and agricultural businesses, there is a greater need to ensure that any potential employee is the right person for the job. Added to that are the provisions of the Equality Act in 2010 (the 2010 Act) that was brought in largely to consolidate the various anti-discrimination laws that were previously passed to minimise discrimination in the workplace.

At the outset, the distinction between a 'self-employed contractor' and a legally defined employee was clarified. In the rural environment, there has been a tradition of using the services of self-employed seasonal contractors particularly in the arable sector of agriculture for, say, ploughing and harvesting. A self-employed person works under the terms of a contract for services whilst an employee receives a contract of employment. Again, in the agricultural sector the nature of engagement of significant numbers of workers is informal.

The distinction is important because of the possible tax implications, issues as to possible vicarious liability when the employer is responsible for a variety of acts by an employee in the course of their employment, and health and safety issues. There are certain other employment-protection rights given by statute, including notably maternity and paternity rights and not to be unfairly dismissed.

When a worker has been engaged regularly over a period of time, his employer should seek advice to ensure that any alleged self-employed status is well founded. There are several tests that will be applied to the facts to see whether the worker is in fact an employee, including the degree of control that is exerted over him or her by the owner of the business. In relation to this book the status of workers will also affect whether they have rights to seek redress for unfair dismissal.

Employers should also be aware of the changes to the 'IR 35' or 'off-payroll' working rules. They are aimed at ensuring that a contractor or worker who provides their services through an intermediary (such as a limited company) would be classed as an employee, if they provided those services directly. In which case, income tax and national insurance contributions must be paid. If the user of the services (the 'client') is a public authority or, from 6 April 2021, a medium to large size business, it has to decide whether the rules apply. If they do, it must account to HM Revenue & Customs for income tax and national insurance contributions via the PAYE system. Otherwise, the intermediary is responsible for accounting to HMRC.

DISCRIMINATION

Employment law was given a major overhaul in 2010 with the passing of the Equality Act, the '2010 Act' referred to above. The aim was to include the various pieces of legislation that dealt with discrimination in the workplace up to that date. The overarching object was to simplify the application of the relevant provisions, and provide a basic framework for protection against direct and indirect discrimination, harassment and victimisation to introduce uniformity. The 2010 Act either repealed or revoked the previous relevant legislation.

The process that was introduced to effect this was identification of nine protected characteristics that are protected by the 2010 Act. These are set out in Sections 4 to 12 and 18 of the 2010 Act. They are:

i.   Age,

ii. Sex,

iii. Race,

iv. Religion and belief (including lack of belief),

v.   Marriage and civil partnership,

vi. Maternity and pregnancy,

vii. Gender reassignment,

viii. Sexual orientation,

ix. Disability.

Case law will continue to develop following the passing of the 2010 Act under its provisions, but the terms and definitions of the previous legislation will still be relevant to its establishment and interpretation.

To protect an employee's rights, there are certain types of prohibited conduct in relation to the protected characteristics mentioned above. The prohibited conduct is set out in the 2010 Act:

i.   Direct discrimination;

ii.   Indirect discrimination;

iii.   Discrimination arising from disability;

iv.   Discrimination relating to gender reassignment – cases of absence from work;

v.   Discrimination relating to maternity and pregnancy;

vi.   Failure to comply with the duty to make reasonable adjustments;

vii.   Harassment;

viii. Victimisation.

Direct discrimination occurs under Section 13 of the 2010 Act when one person is treated less favourably than another in respect of any protected characteristic. It is not sufficient to show that the treatment is different; it has to be less favourable. The 2010 Act sets out various qualifications to this general premise. The test for direct discrimination is objective, that is, was the less favourable treatment because of the protected characteristic in question?

Indirect discrimination occurs under the provisions of the 2010 Act when:

1.   A person (A) discriminates against another (B) if A applies to B a provision, criterion or practice which is discriminatory in relation to a relevant protected characteristic of B's.

2.   For the purposes of subsection (1), a provision, criterion or practice is discriminatory in relation to a relevant protected characteristic of B's if:

(a) A applies, or would apply, it to persons with whom B does not share the characteristic;

(b) it puts, or would put, persons with whom B shares the characteristic at a particular disadvantage when compared with persons with whom B does not share it;

(c) it puts, or would put, B at that disadvantage; and

(d) A cannot show it to be a proportionate means of achieving a legitimate aim.[1]

Unlike direct discrimination, indirect discrimination has the defence of justification as set out in paragraph (d) above.

Harassment was identified under the previous legislation, but under Section 27 of the 2010 Act, if a person 'engages in unwanted conduct related to a relevant characteristic' and the conduct has the purpose of violating a person's personal dignity or creates 'an intimidating, hostile, degrading humiliating or offensive environment'.

The circumstances of the allegation of harassment, the perception of the person raising the allegation and whether it is reasonable for the conduct to have that effect, are all taken into consideration when examining such an allegation.

Victimisation under Section 27 of the 2010 Act occurs if a manager picks on an employee if he or she does a 'protected act', or the person believes that the victim will or has done such an act. A protected act can involve bringing proceedings under the 2010 Act letting another person bring a claim by giving evidence and alleging that the employer has breached the Act.

---

[1] The section also identifies harassment in the context of conduct of a sexual nature.

Direct discrimination can also take place because of a protected characteristic that a person does not personally have. For example, a person can be discriminated against because of their association with someone else who has a protected characteristic, or because they are wrongly perceived to have one, or are treated as if they do. At the time of writing there is little case law on direct discrimination by association.

As explained in more detail below, that in relation to each protected characteristic under the 2010 Act there are common areas which employers should give attention to during the selection process and the course of employment.

In respect of each protected characteristic the prohibited conduct will apply. There will also be in a number of cases the possible justification for certain seemingly discriminatory behaviour if the defence of a 'legitimate aim' can be established. What is set out below is a brief look at the impact of the 2010 Act on each of the protected characteristics.

Age

A person will be discriminated against if they are treated less favourably than another because of their age. Discrimination can be direct and indirect. The situation was affected by the Employment Equality (Repeal of Retirement-Age Provisions) Regulations 2011 which repealed the long-established default age-limits. Both direct and indirect age discrimination are capable of objective justification if they are a proportionate means of achieving a legitimate aim: for example, a company may be able to justify not providing cars to a salesman under 25 because of high insurance costs. An employer may impose a retirement date if they can establish a legitimate aim.

Disability

The effect of the provisions of the 2010 Act relating to disability and discrimination are far-reaching and related not only to employees themselves, but the steps taken by the employer in respect of the work environment to obviate any discrimination. This can be a very difficult process in respect of farms given the nature of the work and the machinery involved. To assist employers and employees in this difficult area the relevant Minister can give guidance as to what is a disability and possible discrimination.

Disability for the purposes of The 2010 Act is defined as 'A person (P) has a disability if:

> (a) P has a physical or mental impairment, and (b) ... their impairment has a substantial and long-term adverse effect on P's ability to carry out normal day-to-day activities.[1]

Schedule 1 of the 2010 Act contains supplementary provisions relating to disability, which can include long-term progressive illnesses like cancer. Long-term is defined as a disability that under Schedule 1 Part 1 will, or is likely to, last for 12 months or more. A 'substantial' disability is one which has a serious adverse effect on a person's ability to do their day-to-day work.

Discrimination therefore can be direct or indirect and, in the case of the latter, employers can avoid a claim of discrimination if they can show a legitimate aim of proportionate means. Under Section 60 of the 2010 Act there are detailed provisions as to what and how a prospective employer can make enquiries about a prospective employee's possible disability and health. This does not prevent employers requesting a pre-employment medical examination; they also can ask questions

---

[1] S.6 Equality Act 2010.

about whether the applicant is able to carry out a job that is 'intrinsic to the work concerned' (The 2010 Act).

Section 20 and Schedule 8 of the 2010 Act require an employer to make adjustments so as to avoid disadvantages caused by disability. These are divided into three requirements which include practical steps to make adjustments to buildings and machinery.

It should be noted that the Equality Act is not confined solely to employment. It also applies to discrimination in the provision of goods, facilities and services or management of premises. The exact nature of these rules is outside the scope of this chapter.

Gender reassignment, marriage and civil partnership, and sexual orientation

There are relatively new provisions prohibiting under Sections 16 and 13 of the 2010 Act discrimination in relation to employees undergoing gender reassignment or because of their married or civil partnership status, or to do with their sexual orientation.

Pregnancy

Discrimination will occur if a woman is discriminated against on the grounds of her pregnancy. Attention should also be paid to the maternity rights and time off work.

Race, religion or belief

With the increased number of migrant workers from the EU, the provisions relating to racial discrimination have become more important in the rural work place. The term 'race' includes colour, nationality, ethnic or national origins; whilst 'religion or belief' covers any religious belief, including atheism. Direct discrimination is commonly obvious in these circumstances but, again, indirect discrimination can be less easy to identify. Here there are exceptions to the regulations where the requirement is to achieve a legitimate aim.

Sex

Unlike sexual orientation mentioned above, this category is to do with the physical status of an employee as a man or woman. There is no defence or justification for prejudice on account of the sex of an employee, but only with regard to indirect discrimination may it be raised as a defence if the reasons are proportionate to achieve a legitimate aim. In the modern workplace there are a number of situations where discrimination could occur, such as refusal to allow a woman to work part-time to facilitate care of her children. Thus, much thought must be given to any decision in the work place that may lead to discrimination on grounds of the employee's sex.

WORK VISAS

Under Sections 15 to 25 of the Immigration, Asylum and Nationality Act 2006 (the 2006 Act), business owners have a statutory duty to carry out checks to confirm if a person has the right to work within the UK. To avoid race-discrimination all workers should be treated the same. The employer sensibly should keep copies of original, acceptable documents before a worker starts work. The rules under the previous legislation apply to workers employed prior to 2008.

It is an offence to fail to check the necessary documents and/or knowingly to employ a worker who is in the UK illegally under the terms of the relevant acts. Failure to comply with the relevant provisions under the 2006 Act and/or knowingly to employ an illegal worker will result in a civil penalty of £20,000 at the time of writing for each illegal worker. Under the criminal jurisdiction, knowingly to employ an illegal worker can on a summary conviction be punished by a maximum fine of £5000 at the time of writing for each worker and/or a term of imprisonment of up to six months. If the case is decided to be heard in a Crown Court, on indictment punishment can be an unlimited fine and/or a prison sentence of up to two years.

The United Kingdom's (UK) exit from the European Union on 31 January 2020 has had a significant effect on the movement of seasonal, and other, workers in agriculture. The UK Government has introduced a number of schemes that are aimed at regulating immigration into the UK. From 1 January 2021 there is a points-based immigration scheme. The criteria that have been set by this scheme mean that a large number of traditional workers' profiles in agriculture would not be able to comply.

Another scheme aimed at helping agriculture in the UK with the possible loss of seasonal workers, when a larger number came from the eastern countries of the EU, is the Seasonal Workers' Scheme. The initial scheme required payment by the worker to join the scheme and to have a requisite amount in their bank account.

Eligible workers who already were living in the UK prior to 31 December 2020, if they satisfied the relevant criteria, can apply for settled status under the EU Settlement Scheme.

THE CONTRACT OF EMPLOYMENT

Because of the informal nature of much of the work on farms, there are situations where there was no written contract of employment, though there would be an enforceable oral contract. Unsurprisingly the exact terms of such an agreement are much more difficult to establish in a tribunal. Section 1 of the Employment Rights Act (1996 Act) provides that no later than two months after the start of employment the employer must give to the employee a written statement of the terms of their employment. If the employer fails to provide a contract the employee can make a complaint to the Employment Tribunal which can decide the terms which should have been included.

Similar to other contracts, there is a distinction between express terms and implied terms. The express terms will be those agreed by the parties to the contract and set out in the contract. These will include inter alia, wages, job description, holiday, hours or work, sick pay and so forth. Implied terms will be looked at in more detail later in this chapter.

There have been a number of statutory controls imposed on aspects of contracts of employment.

Wages

With abolition of the Agricultural Wages Board in 2013 the agricultural sector fell under the terms of the National Minimum Wage Act 1998. The figure for the minimum wage is presently reviewed by the Government every October. Workers who believe that they are being paid below the national minimum wage can bring an action either in an employment tribunal or a local county court. The legal relief would be the difference between what has been paid and the national minimum wage. The body given responsibility for the enforcement of payment of the National Minimum Wage is Her Majesty's Revenue and Customs (HMRC). If HMRC finds that an employer has failed to pay the national minimum wage, they can order the payment of the underpayment and impose a penalty fine. Under the 1996 Act Sections 31–33, it is an offence to fail to pay the national minimum wage, to keep or to falsify records or to obstruct an inspector from HMRC.

Hours and leave

The ability to negotiate hours and holiday leave was available in contracts of employment until 1998, when the Working Time Regulations (WTR) were brought into force. In general terms, the regulations set a working-time limit of an average of 48 hours per week, with special provisions applying to night-time working. Under Regulation 5 of the WTR a worker can agree in writing to work more than 48 hours, but that agreement can be revoked by notice.

Under Regulation 13 of the Working Time (Amendment) Regulations 2007 (WTR), the statutory minimal leave was increased to 5.6 weeks from April 2009: 28 days for employees who work five days per week. Rest-breaks are also provided for under the WTR. In addition, there is a statutory right under the Employment Rights Act 1996 (as amended) to both maternal and paternal parents and dependant's leave. These rights have been revised by the Employment Act 2002 which brought in an amendment relating to maternity leave and pay, and provided for paid paternity leave.

Employee records

As seen above there is a requirement to keep proper records in respect of an employee's wages. Regulations set out the type of information that must be kept and give employees a right to see their records. Employee records whether stored electronically or on paper are subject to the Data Protection Act 1998. This act governs the type of information, which can be stored and allows persons to whom the information relates certain rights of access.

Implied terms

Contracts of employment, like every other contract, are usually the subject of negotiation. In employment the respective bargaining powers of the parties is influential with regard to the contents; combined with the use of standard terms of contract, it means that most salient points are covered. If, however, there is no written contract the parties will have to look to the terms that are implied into the relationship of employer and employee. Unfortunately, they often come to be scrutinised only when there is a dispute. Examples of the types of terms that are implied are the employee's duties of fidelity, obedience and working with due diligence.

An employer also has implied duties under common law to take such steps as are reasonably necessary to ensure the safety of his employees. In addition, there are common law duties, which imply that an employer will provide proper equipment and a safe system of work. If employers fail to attend to the responsibilities of safety that they owe their workers, the employees may consider themselves constructively dismissed and sue for unfair dismissal.

Since safety is a vital part of any employment, there are also statutory obligations imposed on employers by statutes such as the Health and Safety at Work Act 1974 (the 1974 Act) and the Management of Health and Safety at Work Regulations

1999. The Health and Safety Executive was set up by the 1974 Act. There is an Inspectorate whose officers have powers to enter premises, inspect and record any evidence relevant to the enforcement of The 2010 Act. The inspectors have the power to serve an 'improvement notice' on a person or business that they consider to be contravening the provisions of the 1974 Act. The notice will give details of the provision being contravened and specify the period within which the contravention must be remedied. It must also allow sufficient time – 21 days after service on the appellant – for an appeal to be made to an employment tribunal.

The inspector may also serve a 'prohibition notice' on a person who is in control of an activity in which they consider that there is a risk of personal injury. If the risk is imminent, the notice takes effect immediately; in other cases it is deferred. A prohibition can similarly be appealed to an employment tribunal. The tribunal may either cancel or affirm the contents of the notice making such modifications as it thinks fit.

Written particulars of employment

As stated above there is a duty on the part of employers to provide their part or full-time employees with written particulars of employment within two months of the start of their employment. Amongst other things, the statement must identify the parties to the contract, specify the date that employment began and give details of hours of work and remuneration. Details of sick pay and pension-schemes may be contained in some other document, referred to in the written particulars, provided that the other, such as an employment policy document, is reasonably accessible to the employee. It is, however, good practice to ensure that such procedures are established and that employees are aware of them. The employer must notify the employee in writing of any changes to the terms of the contract at the earliest opportunity or not later than one month before the change. It should be noted that generally an employer cannot unilaterally vary the terms of an employment contract.

In cases where terms of a contract of employment are in breach of statutory provisions, the lawful terms take effect as if varied to comply with those provisions. This is so even if illegal terms have been agreed between both parties.

Itemised statements of pay
Under the 1996 Act, every employee has a right to receive an itemised pay statement at or before the payment of wages or salary is made to them. The statement must contain details of the gross amount of wages or salary, the amounts of any variable and any fixed deductions, the net amount of wages or salary payable and, where different parts of the net amount are paid in different ways, the amount and method of payment of each part-payment.

An employee who has not been provided with an itemized pay statement or written particulars – either of the original contract or of changed terms – or who has been provided with a statement that is incomplete or inaccurate, may make a complaint to an employment tribunal. If the tribunal finds that the complaint is valid, it will state the particulars that should have been given, and the employer will be deemed to have given a statement including those particulars.

Breach of employment contract
If the employer is in breach of the terms of the contract of employment, the employee may seek redress by bringing

action against him in the County Court or High Court. The employment tribunal also can award compensation for breach of contract cases up to £25,000.[1]

Discrimination and the course of employment

The discrimination legislation discussed above applies not only to recruitment but to the whole subject of employment; for example, the terms of the contract of employment must not be discriminatory. However, as is evidenced by the passing of the 2010 Act the legislature and, at the relevant time, the law-making bodies of the EU were constantly monitoring and revising the law and regulations surrounding employment. The impact on this area following Brexit is yet to be seen. This is why a small business, as may be typical of a rural agricultural enterprise, needs to seek specialized advice to develop and maintain processes that comply with those rules and regulations.

In general terms, employers should ensure that their treatment of their employees is fair and does not contravene the discrimination laws.

Termination of employment

A contract of employment may be terminated in several ways: by mutual agreement; by 'frustration'; by expiry; by the employee's dismissal either summarily or on notice; by notice of departure given by the employee; by 'constructive dismissal' where the employer's conduct forces the employee to leave; or by a fundamental breach of contract by either the employer or employee. The death of either party, if the employer is an individual, terminates a contract of employment unless, in the case of an employer's death, the contract expressly or by implication provides otherwise, as does the dissolution of a

---

[1] (article 10, Employment Tribunals Extension of Jurisdiction (England and Wales) Order 1994 (SI 1994/1623)

partnership or the winding up of a company; however, the bankruptcy of the employer does not.

'Frustration' of a contract occurs when it becomes impossible for the parties to perform an essential part of the contract. The most usual form is where the contract is frustrated by a long absence of the employee through illness, or if performance of the contract is unlawful, such as when a driver is banned.

Dismissal

If an employee is dismissed, for example without proper notice, he may bring a common-law action for breach of contract. If he is dismissed without proper reason, a statutory action of unfair dismissal may be available. When an employee is dismissed he has a legal entitlement to a written statement of reasons for his dismissal.

Wrongful dismissal

A contract of employment may be ended by notice given by either party. Statute sets out the following minimum periods of notice to which an employee is entitled (as set at the time of writing):

Period of continuous employment	Statutory minimum notice required
0 – 1 month	None
1 month to less than 2 years	1 week
2 to less than 12 years	1 week for each complete year of continuous employment
12 years	12 weeks

When an employee has been continuously employed for one month or more, he must give his employer not less than one week's notice. A longer period of notice to be given by either the employer or the employee may be agreed by the parties. If less than the statutory notice or the agreed notice period is given, the terminating party will be in breach of contract; in the case of an employer giving inadequate notice of termination, the employee will be entitled to bring a case for wrongful dismissal. A case of wrongful dismissal is distinct from a claim of unfair dismissal (see below), although in certain circumstances, the employee may be able to choose which to bring.

Unfair dismissal

The Employment Rights Act 1996 gave an employee the right not to be 'unfairly' dismissed, that is, discharged without a proper process. Dismissal may either be express ('You're fired!'), implied or constructive. An example of the latter type would be a fundamental breach of the terms of the contract by the employer. In this case, the employee may consider themselves as having been dismissed and claim, for example, compensation for unfair dismissal (see below). Constructive Dismissal is however notoriously difficult to prove, as employees have to be able to show that they have been forced to leave their job by their employer's conduct. When an employee is 'let go', they have a legal entitlement to a written statement with reasons for their discharge. Once an employee has established that they have been dismissed, it is for the employer to prove that the reason was fair. The Act sets out situations, which are deemed to be fair; the reason for dismissal must relate to:

- the capability or qualifications of the employee;
- the employee's conduct;

- redundancy (see below);
- statutory prohibition (e.g., if an employee who is engaged as a driver loses his licence, he would contravene the statute if he drove without one); or
- ... some other substantial reason justifying dismissal. If a redundancy situation does not exist, it may be that a dismissal will qualify as fair under this heading if it amounts to a reorganization in the interests of efficiency.

Some reasons for dismissal are deemed to be automatically unfair, for example reasons related to pregnancy or membership of a trade union. Having established that the reason was acceptable, the employer must also show that the way in which they discharged the employee was also fair. For example, if an employer is dismissing on the grounds of conduct, were adequate warnings given and the employee offered an opportunity to improve, before the decision to dismiss was taken? It is only in the event of grave misconduct that an employer may dismiss summarily. In deciding the issue of whether the dismissal is fair, a tribunal will take into account the size of administrative resources of the undertaking, the equity and substantial merits of the case.

The qualifying period for protection from unfair dismissal has varied from six months to two years and has sometimes depended on the size, of the firm. At the time of writing, the requirement is that the employee must have been continuously employed for at least a year if employment commenced prior to April 2012 and thereafter the qualifying period is two years, a requirement that now applies to both full and part-time employees.

In a case where the tribunal finds that the dismissal was unfair, it can make an order for the reinstatement or re-engagement of the complainant or an order for compensation.

An order for reinstatement means that the employee is given the old job back. Before ordering this action, the tribunal has to satisfy itself that it is practicable and that it is fair to the employer. Reinstatement is considered impractical if the employer had to appoint a permanent replacement in order to do the dismissed person's work, or if the employer waited a reasonable time before making the replacement and the dismissed employee did not indicate that he or she wished to be reinstated or re-engaged. The tribunal can also consider the feelings of other staff when deciding on re-employment. When the employee's behaviour contributed to the dismissal, the tribunal might well decide that reinstatement would be unfair.

An order for re-engagement means that the employee is re-employed by the employer but given a different job. This must be suitable, and the terms and conditions should be comparable to those of the employee's old job, unless the complainant contributed to the dismissal, when they need not be.

An award of compensation means that the employer has to pay a cash sum to the employee. This comprises two parts: a basic award and a compensatory award. The basic one is calculated in a similar manner to the calculation of redundancy payments (see below). Thus the longer the person has worked for the employer and the older he or she is, the greater the award. That may be reduced in a case where the tribunal considers that the complainant's conduct contributed to the dismissal. The amount of compensation may be altered depending on whether disciplinary or grievance procedures have been followed.[1] Any redundancy payment that may have been made by the employer to the employee is also deducted from the award. At present, the basic award is subject to a maximum amount which is regularly reviewed.

---

[1] Employment Act 2002.

The compensatory award is intended to cover the employee's losses resulting from his or her dismissal. The losses assessed by the tribunal should include any expenses reasonably incurred by the complainant as a result of the dismissal and loss of any benefits, other than redundancy payments, that he or she may have reasonably expected to enjoy but for the dismissal. The award is subject to a maximum amount except in cases of unfair dismissal which are deemed to be automatically unjust, for 'whistle-blowing' or health and safety reasons. The employee's contributory fault may lead to a reduction in the compensatory award. The employee has a duty to mitigate his or her losses: it must be shown that he or she has actively sought alternative employment, but if the employee refuses an alternative job unreasonably, the award could be reduced. If an offer of reinstatement by the employer is refused no compensatory award is payable.

When an employer refuses to obey an order to re-engage or reinstate the employee, the tribunal must order him or her to pay the basic award and compensatory award plus an additional award of between 26 and 52 weeks' wages. However, if the employer can prove that it is not practicable to comply with the order, because a permanent replacement has been engaged and that it was necessary to do so, the additional amount is not payable.

Grievance procedure
In April 2009 the Employment Act 2008 came into force, which amended the terms of Employment Act 2002. This removed the statutory minimum Disciplinary and Grievance Procedures. These were replaced with a new ACAS code of practice and grievance procedures (the ACAS Code).

The new code is not legally binding like the statutory codes, but when a tribunal looks at the fairness of any dismissal and compensation the implementation of the ACAS Code will be considered. The tribunal can adjust the amount of compensation awarded by up to 25 per cent. The aim of this new code is to make the resolution of grievances and disciplinary matters less confrontational.

Dismissal due to redundancy

The Redundancy Payment Act 1965 introduced the concept of compensation for those workers who lose their jobs through redundancy, irrespective of whether they have another job to go to. These provisions have subsequently been amended and the current law is to be found in the Employment Rights Act 1996. Redundancy is defined as follows: for the purposes of this Act an employee who is dismissed will be taken to be dismissed by reason of redundancy if the dismissal is attributable wholly or mainly to:

a) the fact that his employer has ceased, or intends to cease,

1) to carry on the business for the purposes of which the employee was so employed, or

2) to carry on that business in the place where the employee was so employed, or

b) the fact that the business required,

1) employees to carry out work of a particular kind, or

2) the employee to carry out work of a particular kind in the place where he was so employed, has ceased or diminished or are expected to cease or diminish.[1]

---

[1] Employment Rights Act 1996, s. 139.

In order to qualify for a redundancy payment, the applicant has to have been continuously employed by the employer for a period exceeding two years after his or her eighteenth birthday. Furthermore, if the employer disputes that the applicant was dismissed, or that the reason for dismissal was not redundancy, the onus of proof rests on the applicant.

The continuity of employment is not broken when the employee changes his or her position with the same employer, even though the job itself is different. Nor is it broken by absences from work for reasons of sickness, injury, pregnancy or confinement of less than 26 weeks per year. On 6 April 2006, the revised Transfer of Undertakings (Protection of Employment) came into force and these have been amended by the Collective Redundancies and Transfer of Undertakings (Protection of Employment) (Amendment) Regulations 2014 which govern the extent to which continuity of employment is preserved when a business changes hands. The regulations are complex but it would appear that continuity of employment is preserved when the business is handed over as a going concern and the employee's contract of employment is not terminated by the transferor. The transferee then takes on all the transferor's duties and liabilities to the employee. If the transfer is only of assets and not a transfer of goodwill and customer connection, the transferor is liable for redundancy payments to the employee as the transfer terminates the contract of employment.

Entitlement to a redundancy payment will be lost if the employee unreasonably refuses 'suitable' alternative employment. In order to be suitable, the employment must be with the original employer or an associated employer; it must commence within four weeks of the ending of his or her previous employment and be on the same terms and conditions as the previous contract. If the last point does not hold, the employee must be given a trial period of four weeks in which to decide whether the alternative employment is suitable. It should be noted that even if the job offered is deemed to be suitable, the employee will only lose the right to a redundancy payment if his refusal is unreasonable; what is unreasonable will be judged from the employee's point of view.

There are several different categories of people who are excluded from the right to redundancy payments in addition to those who have unreasonably refused suitable alternative employment. These include employees who are dismissed for misconduct.

The amount of redundancy payment is based upon the employee's age, length of continuous employment and average gross wage.

Age   Redundancy Payment

Age	Redundancy Payment
18-21 years	Half a week's pay for each year of continuous employment
22-40 years	One week's pay for each year of continuous service
41 and above	One and a half week's pay for each year of continuous service

The length of service used in the calculation is subject to a maximum of 20 years. There is a statutory upper limit to the value of a week's pay for the purpose of this calculation, which is index-linked.

In addition to receiving redundancy pay, an employee under redundancy notice is also entitled to time off to look for work.

Once dismissals can be justified on the grounds of redundancy, the employer should select those employees who are to be made redundant in a fair manner. Failure to adopt a fair procedure and apply it in a fair manner may result in claims of unfair dismissal.

VICARIOUS LIABILITY

Should an employee be negligent or commit a crime in the course of his employment, the employer may be found vicariously liable. Thus if a road-traffic accident occurs because of an employee's negligent driving, the employer may be sued for compensation. The principle of 'vicarious liability' only applies in the case of employees, but not in the case of independent contractors whom an employer may have hired. In cases where an employer has exercised care in choosing such contractors and in providing any general supervision, no further liability for their actions will exist.

Check-list of statutory legislation

Collective Redundancies and Transfer of Undertakings
   (Protection of Employment) (Amendment) Regulations 2014
Data Protection Act 1998
Employment Acts 2002, 2008
Employment Appeal Tribunal Rules 1993 (as amended)
Employment Equality (Repeal of Retirement-Age Provisions)
   Regulations 2011
Employment Protection Act 1975
Employment Rights Act 1996 (as amended)
Employment Tribunals Act 1996
Employment Tribunals (Constitution and Rules of Procedure)
   Regulations 2013
Employment Tribunals Extension of Jurisdiction
   (England and Wales) Order 1994
Equality Act 2010
Gangmasters (Licensing) Act 2004
Gangmasters Licensing (Exclusions) Regulations 2013
Health and Safety at Work Act 1974
Human Rights Act 1998
Immigration Act 2016
Immigration, Asylum and Nationality Act 2006
Management of Health and Safety at Work Regulations 1999
National Minimum Wage Act 1998
Redundancy Payment Act 1965
Transfer of Undertakings (Protection of Employment)
   Regulations 2006
Working Time Regulations 1998
Working Time (Amendment) Regulations 2007, 2009

Non-statutory
ACAS Code of Practice and Grievance Procedures 2009

Index

About the Author

Peter Morris LLB (Hons), PGCHE, is a non-practising solicitor, and Farmers' Club Scholar. He is Senior Lecturer in Law at the Royal Agricultural University, Cirencester, in the School of Equine Management and Science.